# Grow
## Your Property Management
# Business

Fourandhalf's Guide
To Growing Your Property Management Business

Copyright © 2014 by Fourandhalf

ISBN-13: 978-0-692-22690-2

# Grow

## Your Property Management

# Business

## By Fourandhalf.com

Internet Marketing for
Property Management Companies

*Introducing...*

# Fourandhalf's Guide to Growing Your Property Management Business

Besides being the only Internet Marketing company working exclusively with Property Management firms, Fourandhalf researches and writes on the latest Strategies, Technologies and Marketing tips to help Property Managers grow their businesses.

Our passion is to help small businesses succeed in the digital age and this guide is designed to provide a digital marketing road map for Property Management industry business owners and executives.

If you are looking to grow your property management company and acquire more properties under your management portfolio, this guide is for you.

To get the latest Property Management Strategy tips, sign up for our weekly blog: fourandhalf.com/technology-blog

# Contents

# Why Write This Book?

We put this book together as a tool for professionals who know a lot about property management but maybe not so much about Internet marketing.

Our access to the latest marketing strategies and the newest Internet technologies will help you grow your business and close your leads with simple steps.

Fourandhalf aims to offer suggestions and solutions that will help you bring more landlords and real estate investors to your property management business.

Take a look at this *Guide to Growing your Property Management Business*, share it with your colleagues and then if you have any questions or thoughts about what you can gain with an increased focus on your Internet marketing strategies, please feel free to get in touch.

info@fourandhalf.com
510-889-9921

# What is Internet Marketing?

Not only does the phrase "Internet Marketing" mean a lot of different things, but it's changing all the time. Staying up to date with how search engines work, what Google plans to do next and how to get the right people paying attention to your blog takes knowledge and expertise. Here are just a few things that make up Internet Marketing:

- » Video Blogs
- » Social Media
- » Google AdWords
- » Search Engine Optimization
- » Online Reviews
- » Websites
- » Pay-Per-Click Advertising

It's not enough to have a Facebook page or a good looking website. You need to present yourself as an expert in property management, and you need to show potential clients why you stand out from all the other management companies in your area.

# Why in the World Should I Read this Book?

» Because I want more clients.
» Because I am a great property manager, and not enough people know
» Because being ahead of the technological curve is important.
» Because my future client just inherited a house and needs my help
» Because I'm too busy to spend a lot of time marketing my business.
» Because it's short!
» Because property managers can lose up to 30% of their portfolio every year
» Because my competitors have more online reviews than me.
» Because I think Internet marketing is expensive or out of my league or for other people.
» Because I've tried this type of marketing before and nothing good happened.
» Because Google+ frustrates the hell out of me.

**Because I need to know.**

# What Can I Expect from this Book?

Fame and fortune, mostly.

Actually, that's not true. We cannot make you rich, happy, famous or thin.

We can, however, give you the tools and resources necessary to grow your property management business. We can show you how to approach the Internet for all your marketing needs. By the time you've finished reading this guide, you'll have a better understanding of how to:

- » Attract more business
- » Manage your sales leads
- » Close those sales leads
- » Record videos that answer landlord questions
- » Manage content marketing
- » Create a super sales landing page
- » Advertise on Facebook
- » Use Google AdWords
- » Maximize your social media presence
- » Ask for positive online reviews

Don't worry – we won't tell you what to do and then leave you hanging. We'll give you specific instructions for how to execute an Internet marketing plan that attracts more business for property managers.

Let's grow your property management business

# Chapter 1
# The Goal

Any time you think about investing in marketing strategies for your property management business, you have to start from the value of a contract.

Think about what one property management contract means for you and your business. When you have a specific dollar figure to work with, you can be a lot more strategic when deciding what to spend and how to advertise.

For our purposes, we're going to use basic math to establish the value of a management contract. You can add or subtract to our standard figures to meet your own averages.

## Sample Contract Value

Monthly Management Fee:  $100

12 months:  $1,200 annual income from one property

We're also assuming the average client will stay with you for three years. Again – this might seem either low or high to you, but let's say you have that $1,200 annual contract for three years. That gives you a three-year total of $3,600 for one managed property.

Most property managers have a lease up fee, or some other cost charged to clients. In order to make our math nice and even, let's say your lease up fee on this contract is $400. When all is said and done, that means a single contract is worth $4,000 to you.

One property = $4,000.

## Increasing Business

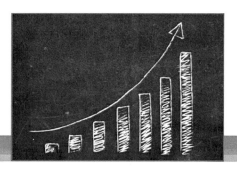

Now that you know the value of your contract, how much new business do you want to attract? It depends on your internal capacity.

Here are 3 key questions to ask:

> » Do I have the property managers, leasing agents and support staff to handle a modest increase in business or a huge increase in business?
> » Is my technology up to date and able to handle additional properties?
>> » Hint: If you're using an Excel spreadsheet to track income and expenses on the properties you manage, you might want to upgrade to more sophisticated software system before increasing your workload.
> » Who is my ideal client and what does my ideal property management contract look like?

## Set a Goal

Things we know:

> » How much a contract is worth to you; and,
> » How much extra business you can handle.

Now, it's time to set a goal. Make it a specific goal so you know what you're working towards and how to put together your Internet marketing strategy.

~ Maybe your goal is one new property per week or sixty-five a month.

~ Maybe you want to close two new sales leads this month and then four next month and then six the month after that.

Don't worry about *how* you're going to do it. We'll get to that in a few pages.

Right now, you only have to set that goal.

## Investment

Now it's time to decide how much money you want to invest in your marketing strategy. We know that one contract is worth $4,000. How much can you spend to ensure you make that $4,000?

Some property managers will spend thousands; others with spend hundreds. Your success does not depend on **what** you spend; it depends on **how** you spend.

DON'T spend thousands of dollars the wrong way – you may not get a single property management contract out of it.

DO spend what you can the right way – you'll be surprised at the results you attract.

Not sure how much to spend? That's okay. Once you've read up on the marketing options available to you, come back and decide.

We can tell you that in our years of helping lots of property management companies with their marketing budgets, we know that the average property management contract for a single family house is gained after an investment of between $100 and $500.

This is an average range.

You might have to spend a little more; you may be able to spend a little less. Based on our experience, to get that one contract worth $4,000, you should be prepared to spend between $100 to $500 on marketing.

# Chapter 2
## Self-Assessment

Understanding where you are is essential to charting a path to your new destination.

It's time for a self-assessment.

This won't be too painful. All you have to do is take a hard, objective look at what you're currently doing to attract new business. Which of these are you presently doing?

___Print Ads          ___Email blasts          ___Brochures

___Radio Ads          ___Cold Calling          ___Billboard Ads

___Direct Mail          ___Events          ___Presentations

How are these things working for you?

That's what we thought.

What about these? Are you doing any of these things?

___Pay-Per-Click                    ___Facebook Advertising

___Blogs                            ___Google AdWords

___Videos                           ___Online Reviews

___Content Marketing                ___SEO

___Google+

These are the marketing strategies that we have seen get results. They don't have to be expensive and they don't have to be difficult.

You are looking for the marketing strategies that will establish your company as the property management experts in your service area. They are focused and strategic and they will get you results.

## Lead Management

Just as important as your marketing strategies is your lead management system. If people are calling your office or sending emails from your website and you aren't tracking or following up, you are missing out on a lot of potential business. Know how to track those leads, know where they are coming from and know how to turn them into contracts.

For tips on closing leads skip to Chapter 5, Closing the Deal or head over to our blog at www.fourandhalf.com/technology-blog.

Chapter 3
# Planning your Marketing Strategy

## Social Media Presence

It's important to have a presence on social media but more important than your presence is your purpose.

Think about who you are and who you aren't.

You ARE a professional property management company looking to attract new business from local landlords and real estate investors.

You ARE NOT an art gallery or a musician hoping to have your creations go viral.

You ARE an expert in subjects like leases, tenant screening, property inspections and evictions.

You ARE NOT trying to win a popularity contest.

The quantity of your "likes" and "follows" on sites like Facebook and Twitter are far less important than the quality of the people in your social network. If you have 500 people liking your Facebook page, that's great. However, if the majority of those likes are from people out of state who do not own rental properties, you're not going to get much more business.

On the other hand, if you have only 200 people liking your company's Facebook page and most of them are real estate investors, landlords or even tenants in your local service area looking for property, property management or simple advice, you've got a much better shot at closing a new deal.

You are never supposed to use social media as the central strategy for growing your business. This is not the correct approach for property managers. If you are hoping to set up a Facebook page and promote your Twitter account and then sit back and wait for the business to come to you, you will be very disappointed with the results.

The purpose of social media is to amplify your content.

This is the key, so we're going to repeat it:

The purpose of social media is to amplify your content.

You have to have high quality content, and social media can help you magnify your message. We'll talk more about content in the next section. Right now, we want you to understand that your Facebook page and your Twitter page and your Google+ page are meant to supplement the more important areas of your marketing strategy.

Building your brand is another way social media can help you. Property management companies want a presence that is professional, organized and categorized. The goal is to ensure people will know who you are and what you do when they find you on Facebook, Twitter and Google+.

The purpose is to set up your profile properly, represent your business consistently and provide good content. Your business will increase because of your targeted marketing and because of your educational articles and videos. Building a trust factor with your audience will lead to more property management contracts.

So remember:

> » Using social media as the sole source of new business acquisition is not going to work. You don't want to invest all your resources there.
> » The center of all things marketing is your content. Social media is only the amplifier of that content. It's a valuable tool and a valid vehicle that you should be using, but your content is really what you want to focus on.

## Content Marketing

So what is this thing we call CONTENT?

We mean information. Education. Facts, figures and advice presented in a way that's easy for your audience to understand.

We mean videos.

We mean blogs.

We mean help.

Your clients call and email you on a daily basis with questions. They want to know whether they should allow pets in their rental properties. They ask about what to do when the rent is late. Investors have questions about what type of properties are best for the rental market. Landlords managing their own homes might inquire about the best upgrades to make and how to stay on top of preventative maintenance issues.

Start keeping track of these questions that come in. Whenever you are ready to film/write your next blog, all you have to do is to pick one of the questions from the list and answer it.

Your blogs don't have to be long. They simply have to solve a problem for your potential clients. They should demonstrate that you know what you're talking about and they have to spark the idea that you can make property management a whole lot easier for whoever is asking the questions.

For example, let's say you get a phone call from someone who wants to know how you market the properties you manage. You don't have to do a lot of digging to answer the question.

You can tell the person about all the websites you list properties on, how you take professional photos and detailed videos that really capture the best parts of the property.

You talk about the signage you might use and what kind of information you always include in your listings.

In about five minutes you have answered that question expertly and efficiently. You now also have an excellent blog post that can reach potential new clients. People are searching for this information online, and when your blog comes up with the answer, you are the company they are going to call.

Did we mention your content has to be good? We all know what bad content looks like. We've seen it. Your content needs to stand apart and be:

- » Original
- » Educational
- » Informative
- » Intelligent

No one is going to waste their time watching a video or reading a blog that is poorly written, unprofessional and too caught up in self-promotion.

Sure, you can let people know what your property man-agement company does and what sets it apart from others. But your content isn't intended to deliver a hard sales pitch. It's to establish your company as the expert in property management. It's to help people solve their property management problems.

Your audience is smart, thoughtful and they likely have done their homework. They might be landlords who have successfully managed properties themselves, but are ready to turn it over to professionals and they want to make sure they choose the best in the business. They might be "accidental landlords" who inherited a property they have no idea how to care for. Or, they might be people who know they can manage the day-to-day elements of a rental property but have no idea how to go about finding and screening a tenant, or writing up a lease.

Remember: When you are able to identify the pain points experienced by landlords and real estate investors and then solve those problems – they'll be a lot more interested in working with you, and a lot less interested in doing property management themselves.

Your content is yours forever. You write your blogs, you produce your videos and then you send that content out into the Internet world for people to find online when they're researching for information.

Let's say you write a blog about Fair Housing Laws in San Francisco. A landlord might do an Internet search for those keywords because she's renting out a house and she doesn't want to violate any Fair Housing laws with her advertising or her screening process.

Guess whose blog is going to come up when she does her Google search?

Yours.

That landlord will read your blog or watch your video and realize that you know a lot more about fair housing than she does. She may also realize that there's a lot more involved in tenant screening and landlord/tenant law than she's willing to learn. She's not going to spend a lot of time searching for property management companies. She's already found a good one. You are the first call she's going to make.

A little bit earlier, we were talking about the proper use of social media. We said Facebook and Twitter and Google+ are great tools to have in your marketing toolbox, but they have to be used properly. We also told you that one of the main purposes of your Facebook page and Twitter account are not to attract as many followers as possible or engage with your audience in the form of retweets and likes. Instead, it's to AMPLIFY YOUR CONTENT. Use those pages to share your content.

## Online Reputation

Your online reputation is critical.

Active reputation management is essential in the property management industry because as you know, tenants review property managers only when there is a problem.

For example, when you are in the process of an eviction, which is an act required by law when a tenant does not pay rent, that tenant is likely to write a negative review about you. Tenants who have to wait for repairs and services while you try to get authorization from an owner are also likely to write something negative about you and your services.

In the property management business, you might manage 300 units in a single year, and perhaps you will get four to five reviews in that year. Most of them, unfortunately, will be negative.

But it doesn't have to be that way!

Why not?

Because within that same year, you will come into contact with at least 800 people. Maybe even 1,000. Think about all the owners, tenants, roommates and vendors you work with. All these people can give you a positive review, but they probably won't think about doing it unless you ask.

If you want to gain new property management business, you cannot allow the small minority of your tenants to represent your business online to the whole world.

Getting more reviews needs to be a marketing priority for you. If you want to be a bigger property management company, or more importantly, if you are a small property management company that wants to look like a larger company, get more online reviews.

Potential clients cannot necessarily see the number of properties you manage when they look for you online, but if they go to Yelp or Google+ or some other review site and see your reviews there, it will have an impact.

Think about it: who looks more successful – a company with 17 positive reviews, even if they only have 50 proper-ties, or a company with just 3 positive reviews and perhaps 1,000 properties? The company with 17 reviews will look bigger and better. That will help you, so solicit your reviews and get some glowing ones that will balance out the negative reviews that all companies inevitably receive, no matter how good they are at what they do.

Remember: There is no magic bullet in online reputation management for property managers. You will come across companies that offer you reviews put together by people other than owners and tenants; people you have never even met or talked to. They will publish those positive reviews on your sites.

We strongly advise against this type of service.

First of all, the reviews are bogus and don't actually reflect anything you do. Secondly, Yelp and Google use ever-evolving algorithms to track the reviews. If they find that a company is posting fake reviews on your behalf, the account will likely be shut down. That would be a huge problem for your business and detrimental to your reputation. It will also cost you money, so don't take the chance.

Instead of taking what seems like an easy way to a great online reputation, simply ask your clients for reviews, which we'll tell you how to do in the Execution chapter of this guide. When you do this, your positive reviews will increase and your good work will be accurately reflected online.

## Landing Page

We're learning about all the important tools and techniques that Internet marketing provides property managers; branding, proper usage of social media, positive reviews, and content.

Right now we're going to focus on your landing page.

A landing page is the place that you take your visitors when they click on an ad or a link you might include in your blogs or on your social networking sites. Your landing page needs to be clear and thorough, and it needs to give your visitors a reason to contact you for more information.

A landing page needs to be your best Sales Person.

We always recommend you have a video on your landing page. That video might feature you talking about what sets your property management company out in front of your competition. It might be your latest informational blog. Maybe it's a current landlord talking about the difference you're making in the way his property is maintained.

Have a brief video on your landing page that introduces visitors to who you are and what you do.

*The above sample page shows the various elements that make up a good Landing Page. The purpose of the Landing Page is to convince your website visitors that you are the right solution to their problems. The page needs to be dedicated to showcasing all the right reasons why a landlord should choose your property management company:*

> » *Initial Hook or special offer to get people interested*
> » *Clear Value Proposition*
> » *A Video on why use your company*
> » *Client Testimonials*
> » *A detailed Service Overview explained in terms of benefits, not features*

There should be a Call to Action on your landing page as well. This tells the visitor what to do. Some examples of a good Call to Action are:

Contact Us Today

Follow Us on Facebook

Call for a Free Quote

Email Us for Details

Save 10% on a Two-Year Contract

Read Our Customer Reviews

Watch How We Conduct a Video Inspection

Ask About Eviction Protection

The final element of your landing page must be a way for visitors to contact you.

Always give them several different options. Provide an email address and a phone number. Leave a contact form they can fill out. Make it easy for them to take the next step, and you'll be that closer to landing a new property management contract.

## Advertising

It's time to use the A-word.

Advertising.

We're not talking about a 30-second television spot or a billboard. When you use advertising like that, you aren't able to target your audience. Advertising on the Internet gives you the ability to reach only the types of consumers who would be interested in your services: local landlords and real estate investors.

We'll start with Google AdWords, or as it might be called, Google Pay-per-Click. You don't have to be an Internet expert to know about Google. A majority of people use

Google to search for information and answer questions they might have.

To advertise with Google AdWords, you need to bid on specific keywords that you believe your ideal client will be using. For example, if you are a property management company in Sacramento, your best keywords will be "Sacramento property management." Those are the keywords a landlord in your area might type into Google while looking for services. When that landlord does perform this Google search, you want your website and your landing page to be one of the best options to click.

This can be an expensive strategy, so you'll have to go back to the early part of this guide and revisit what you decided to invest in advertising and marketing.

Google AdWords are getting more expensive because more companies have realized the power behind these keywords, and there is more competition for clicks.

We told you that our experience has shown most property management contracts cost between $100 and $500 to close. This isn't a cost-per-lead quote; this is the average AdWords cost for one client, in other words, closing one new property management contact.

It might work out even better for you. Your $1000 spent on Google AdWords could end up bringing in 10 new management contracts. That's something to celebrate. On the other hand, your $1000 investment could bring you a few potential leads that just don't work out.

As we've been saying, quality is a lot more important than quantity. If you decide to do a Google AdWords campaign, you would rather gain 20 quality leads instead of 50 terrible leads.

There are SEO companies out there and even some property managers who try to launch their own AdWords campaigns that are stumbling over this very pitfall. It's easy to bid on a bunch of keywords that you think will make sense, but if you're not strategic about your audience or you don't really understand the property management business, you could end up with the wrong leads.

For example, look at these two keywords. It won't take you long to figure out which is the better option.

"San Diego rental homes"

"San Diego rental homes management"

Which set of keywords would work best for you? If you use the first one, "San Diego rental homes," you might end up with 200 tenants in the San Diego area clicking to your site in the hopes of finding a home. That might work for you if your goal is to find tenants.

However, if your goal is to find landlords and real estate investors who need property management, the second set of keywords, "San Diego rental homes management" will get you leads that are better in quality. You might not get as many leads, but all the leads you do get are your ideal clients.

Achieving a proper return on your investment when it comes to Google AdWords requires a strategic campaign that is set up and launched properly. It also needs to be monitored heavily. Weed out the keywords that are not bringing you the right potential clients.

Google AdWords can be a useful marketing strategy for property managers. At Fourandhalf, we always advise our clients to look at it as an adrenaline shot instead of the foundation of your advertising. When you use this type of advertising campaign strategically and sparingly, it can give you a quick jolt of new business.

Facebook offers a targeted advertising campaign that most property managers will find a bit more affordable, and it can be a successful way to introduce potential clients to your company. All you need to create an ad is a

Facebook business page. Create your ad with any text, videos or pictures you want. Come up with something that will grab the attention of the landlords and investors you are trying to reach.

Once you complete the creation of your ad on Facebook, the real work starts. Facebook will help you set parameters for who sees that ad. You can narrow down your audience so you know that every dollar you are spending on Facebook advertising is used to reach exactly the people you want to reach.

You'll choose the U.S. as your country and then you'll choose the exact city or cities of your service location. If you're a property management company in Jacksonville, you'll set your geographic area as Jacksonville, Florida and maybe anyone living within 25 or 30 miles of Jacksonville. After you define your radius, you can continue to tighten up your profile. Select the age group you want toreach, gender and precise interests, such as real estate investing.

What does this Facebook ad get you?

Let's say you are that Jacksonville property management company. Instead of spending your advertising dollars reaching a million people that are unlikely to bring you any new properties to manage, you spend $75 to run a targeted Facebook ad that might reach 1,500 landlords and real estate investors within 25 miles of Jacksonville. Out of those 1,500 people who saw the ad, you might get 50 engagements. By "engagements," we mean 50 people might "like" your Facebook page or play the video that you post with the ad.

Even getting one new property management contract out of those numbers will more than pay for the Facebook ad.

# Chapter 4
# Execution

We've given property managers some great ideas on how to develop an Internet marketing strategy that works.

So, how do you get started?

If you're tired of reading, you can contact us right now and we'll take care of it for you.

Or, you can keep reading and learn how to execute a solid marketing plan on your own. We're only a phone call or an email away if you run into trouble or need help.

To put your simple marketing and advertising plan into place, you'll need to develop content and you'll need to create the right platforms for that content. At a minimum, you must have:

- » A Facebook page
- » A Google+ page
- » Videos and blogs
- » Positive online reviews

Let's get started.

## Rent-Ready Facebook Pages

As a professional property manager, you are always stressing the importance of making sure a rental home is "rent-ready," meaning it is fit to hit the market. We feel the same way about your Facebook page. Don't set one up until you're ready to post all the pictures, videos and information that you need. You don't want potential new clients to see a work in progress.

Start with a great profile picture. Ideally, you have a photo of your logo that can easily be cropped into a square and posted as your profile picture. Remember, you want to be consistent and easily identifiable. Save the school pictures for your personal page. On your property management business page, you need a clear, professional and easy to see logo as your profile picture.

You can be a little more creative with your cover photo. Just be sure it makes sense. For example, if you're a property management company in Las Vegas, posting a tropical beach scene as your cover photo is going to confuse visitors. Show a landmark or an easily recognized structure from your service area. Post some city pride.

The rest of the information should be as detailed as possible. Provide your phone number, website, an email address and a brief description of who you are and what you do. You can list your hours, advise people on where to park when they come to your office, and even include pricing and service information.

Once your Facebook page is live, remember the purpose. You are on Facebook to share your content, establish your brand and appeal to landlords and real estate investors who can benefit from your property management services.

## Managing Google+

Even the most Internet savvy property manager can easily get tripped up by Google+. Its features and requirements always seem to be changing, and at Fourandhalf we often find ourselves turning to our in-house Google experts for help. You need to get a grip on it, because Google+ is an essential tool for your Internet marketing strategy. You'll have a hard time growing your property management business without it.

If you're not familiar with Google+, think of it as an updated and digital re-creation of the yellow pages. It provides the same service to a local business by providing a category and a specific location for what you do and where you are. When your property management business is on Google+, anyone searching for a company like yours in your local area will be able to find you. For example, if a landlord in San Francisco is looking for a local company to manage some properties and he searches Google for "San Francisco Property Management," those companies will show up in the Google search results.

Not only will your company's name pop up, there will also be a map pinpointing the locations of the property management companies that came up in the search. If you're a San Francisco property management company, you'll want to make sure you're on that map. To get on the map, you need a Google Local page with a verified address. You also need to properly categorize your business so it shows up in searches.

At least that's the plan. Often there are more property management companies than there are available pins on the Google map.

So how do you make sure you're there?

That depends on Google. And as we all know – Internet technology is constantly changing.

There are ways to increase your chances, however. We know with total certainty that if you want front page placement for free on Google, you have to connect your Google Local listing with a Google+ Business Page. More importantly, you have to make sure your profile is complete.

A complete Google+ profile includes:

» Business description
» Correct business categorization
» Verified address and phone number
» Links to your website
» Photos and images
» Links to your YouTube channel

Sounds like a lot of work.

But it's worth the time and attention because all of your reviews, videos and other company information are there in one place. You boost your visibility and your SEO and you do it all in one location that almost anyone can find.

Google has recently combined a number of its features into the Google+ product. It's meant to be user-friendly and similar to other popular spots like Yelp, Facebook, MapQuest and Yahoo Local. Don't be intimidated. There have been a few concerns some businesses have raised, and we work with clients all the time to better manage their Google+ listings. Here are a few things to watch out for:

> » Your business address is old. If you created your Google Places page two years ago when you had a different address, Google will mail its verification to the old address.
> » There is no address. You can run into trouble if you don't have a physical location or you have more than one.
> » Someone else set you up. If a third party got your Google Places account going with a non-Google email address, verification may be difficult because Google+ will require a Gmail address or an email account from Google Apps.
> » A password left with an employee. If the person who set up your Google+ page has left and no one else knows the password, you'll have trouble activating your account.

A little legwork is required to work these issues out. Sometimes, you even need to call Google. Don't worry. They're very nice.

## Blogs and Videos

As we said earlier, you have no shortage of material to talk about for your blogs. We always recommend a combined video and blog. You can easily record yourself talking about a particular topic and then you can provide a written blog for people to refer to after they've watched your video. Some of the most popular blog topics our property management clients have chosen to discuss include:

- » Inspections
- » Tenant Screening
- » Pet Policies
- » How to Choose an Investment Property
- » How to Handle Late Rent Payments
- » Avoiding Eviction
- » How a Property Manager Handles Maintenance
- » Marketing Rental Properties
- » Reducing Vacancy
- » Setting the Right Rental Price
- » How a Property Manager Handles Finances
- » Getting your Property Ready for the Rental Market
- » Managing Vendors and Contractors

Make sure your blogs are easy to understand, informative and free of any spelling or grammar errors. Your goal is to establish yourself as an expert. You can't do that if your written blog does not make sense.

Putting together a video might seem complicated, but it's not.

We've got some step-by-step instructions that will help you make your own video. We use iPhones and iPads when we record video blogs for our clients and for our own content. You probably have one of these devices, they take good video and the file format they use is really easy to edit and send to YouTube.

There are a few things you need in order to make a pro-fessional, high quality video:

Thing 1: A good location. Record your video in a quiet place with plenty of light. Try to find a private office or room so you can close the door.

**Thing 2: Equipment.**  You will need your iPhone or your iPad with plenty of room on it for videos. If your device is full of vacation photos and your favorite music, you might have to erase some. A video will take about 100Mb per minute, so calculate how much you'll need on your device.

**Thing 3: Chargers.**  Keep your charging cable close because you never know when you'll need it. You can charge it and transfer video off of the iPhone or the iPad if you start running out of room.

**Thing 4: Airplane Mode.**  Set your phone or iPad to airplane mode. You don't want to be interrupted while you're shooting.

**Thing 5: Mounting.**  Get a mount to attach the iPhone or the iPad to a tripod. Each mount is different and you can purchase them for as little as $20 or $30 on Amazon. Make sure you get the right size.

**Thing 6: Microphone.**  If you're in a loud place, or you're concerned with the quality of audio on your blog, a good option is to get a microphone. You can find microphones that plug right into your phone or your iPad. There are also professional microphones that you can use, but you'll need a preamp to attach the microphone to your device. Don't forget a stand with your microphone. It's okay to hold a microphone when it's just you, but if you're interviewing someone, it's awkward to be on the video holding your microphone.

Now that you have everything you need, it's time to set up.

1.      Keep the camera close to you. The camera should already be set to video. The screen will show two different things depending on whether it's set to picture or video. If you start at the picture setting and then move it over to video, you're not going to get the same quality and you may not even be in the frame.

2.      Position the camera just below your eyes. You don't want to see everything that's behind you in the video. We don't want too much headroom because we want you to be the center of the blog. It also helps your audio to sound better when you have the camera in the right place.

3.      Use the rear-facing camera. Don't use the camera side that has the image on it or the screen. The rear camera has a higher resolution. Also, people tend to look at the image in the picture instead of at the camera. We don't want you to be looking off to the side; we want you looking right at the camera.

4.      Keep your notes on the table. If you have cue cards held up, you tend to look off to the side so you can read them. It won't look right on the video. Looking down to check your notes is a natural look and it doesn't look like you're staring off into space.

5.        Have someone stand behind the camera if you're nervous or a little camera shy. It can help you feel like you're talking to that person instead of talking to the camera.

There are a few things you want to think about while you are shooting. Here are three specific tips:

Turn off the camera between takes. If someone is uploading the video, then having a big file is trouble. You want to keep those files as small as possible. The easiest way to do that is to make sure you shut it off between takes. You also have the opportunity to erase a bad take. That will save you room on your phone.

Pause when you need to. Just stop if you screw up or made a mistake. Start at an earlier sentence and you'll have a good place to stop when you're editing. Always pause when you start and pause when you're done. Don't keep talking as you're getting up to shut off the camera. It doesn't look right. Think about a newscast. You see that point when the newscasters are chatting with each other before the whole segment cuts off.

Have an intro and an outro. Start with who you are, who you work for and what you want to talk about. When you're done, it helps to say something like this:

"Thanks for listening. My name is Beth and if you have any questions, please feel free to contact us at Beth Smith Property Management."

Once you have your video put together and your blog written up, it's time to share that information with the Internet. Post it on your own site and share it on your social media platforms.

## Positive Online Reviews

We told you earlier that online reviews could give potential clients an idea of how you do business and what your current and former customers think about your work. We also said that negative reviews are inevitable, and you need to offset them with a larger number of overwhelming positive reviews. How do you do that? The answer is easy:

*The secret to online reputation management is this: you have to ask.*

When it comes to handling "the ask" effectively, there are only two things to keep in mind.

1.  You must make it simple.

2.  You must make it timely.

## Make it Simple

First, you need to decide where you want your review posted. Pick your platform, whether it is Google, Yelp, Yahoo or some other site. We often recommend Yelp and Google to our clients because those are the most widely read and the most accessible.

Set your property management business up on these sites, and display all the branding and imaging that reflects your company and what you do. Be consistent, because it's important that you are easily recognizable. When your pictures and logo as well as your company description are in order, your tenants and owners will know it is you when they arrive at the review site. This makes it easy for them to post their review, and they don't have to do a lot of digging or research trying to find you.

## Make it Timely

Ask for a review at a point when you know your tenant or owner is the happiest. Send an email asking for a review when you know your relationships are strong and your contacts are pleased with the work you are doing. The best times to ask a tenant for a review might be after a successful repair or after you issue a full security deposit at move out. An owner might be willing to write a great review for you once a superb tenant renews a lease or you save money on maintenance costs. Time the ask at a point you know you will get an encouraging and positive review.

# Chapter 5
## Closing the Deal

Your marketing plans have done their job when you start to see new sales leads rolling in. All of the great marketing in the world is going to be pointless if you cannot close the deal. You won't gain extra property management business just by marketing and advertising your services. You have to close the deals.

Now's the time to examine your sales process and your lead management system.

**Do you know where your leads are coming from?**

When you put your content out there and list contact information on your landing page, what phone number are you providing? Which email address?

You need to know this so you can be consistent and follow up quickly. You might provide an office phone number or your cell phone number on your landing page. The Contact Form that a lead fills out on your site goes to a specific email inbox. You need to check it regularly.

This is important because some of us don't answer calls from unfamiliar numbers on our cell phones. However, if your cell phone number is out there as a way to contact your property management company, you better be willing to answer it every time it rings.

Check the email inbox that leads respond to. Don't leave emails in there for days and weeks. Check it constantly so you can respond to leads right away.

Put a 10-minute rule in place.

You want to get in touch with a lead within 10 minutes of their first contact. This is crucial. You might not be able to pick up the phone at the exact moment they call, but call them back as soon as you listen to their message or get to a place you can talk.

Our research shows that you have an 80 percent chance of talking to that lead if you call them back within 30 minutes of their contact. If you wait any longer, your chances of getting in touch begin to dwindle. They lose interest, they call someone else or they forget about you altogether.

Follow up 3 Times

After the initial phone call or email, follow up with your lead. We recommend doing at least three follow ups within the first week you find the lead. Each touch should include both a phone call and an email. This is essential because the person who has contacted you might not be ready the first time you talk. They might be thinking about it, or they might be talking to other property managers. You want to show that lead how much you want their business. Touch each lead at least three times during your follow up within seven days, and use phone calls and email.

## Month-end Close

At Fourandhalf, we start calling everyone at the end of the month. If you've considered working with us before, you might remember that you heard from us at the end of the month we first talked. If you ever submitted a form or talked to us at a conference, you surely heard from us, and you should use the same strategy for your business. Right before the end of the month, go through all your old leads and check your email forms and phone calls. Touch every single lead before the month ends. Offer a deal. Entice them to use your services.

This means working really hard at the end of every month. It's your job, and I know it requires eight to 10 hours of work every day. It includes rejection and hearing "no" and leaving voicemail messages. However, there is a payoff. The strategy works well and if all of your marketing is in place and your sales process has included immediate response and active follow ups, you'll find yourself with more property management business at the end of each month.

# Chapter 6
## What Now?

At this point, you should feel pretty confident about how to grow your property management business using the Internet marketing strategies we've proposed and developed. It's a lot to digest and we recommend you do two things to make sure it's successful. We recommend you get professional help and you measure your success.

## Professional Help

At Fourandhalf, we are always sharing tips and tools with property managers so they know how to best market themselves and attract new clients. If there's something you think we have not covered, get in touch with us. You can also review our blogs on different marketing topics and meet some of the partners we work with to make your job a little easier.

http://fourandhalf.com/technology-blog/

If you are currently managing your own marketing and advertising strategies, and you feel like you've gained some useful information in this guide, we're sure you'll feel comfortable taking your property management business to the next step. Try some of the things we talked about, and let us know what worked for you and what didn't. We'd love to hear your feedback.

If you like most of what you've read, but you're a little unsure of doing all this yourself, especially with a growing list of properties to manage, don't be afraid to ask for help. Give us a call or send us an email and we'll make you feel more comfortable with Internet marketing and take you through some of the best options for your company right now.

http://fourandhalf.com/
property-management-marketing/

If you're still not sold on things like content management and Google+, we understand. Take it slow. Follow some of the other companies that are doing it, and see what you think of their progress.

# What Does Success Look Like?

The obvious answer is more property management contracts. When you win more business, you know your marketing plan is working. We don't want you to get too comfortable, though. Even the best Internet marketing strategies need constant management and measurement. Take advantage of Google and Facebook analytics so you know exactly what kind of volume you're getting and use that information to turn visitors into clients. Keep setting new standards for yourself and track your record of improvement so you know what's working and what still needs work.

Thanks for taking the time to read *Fourandhalf's Guide to Growing Your Property Management Business*. We hope it's been helpful, and we hope to hear from you soon.

Made in the USA
San Bernardino, CA
23 September 2015